W9-BNY-810

THIS JOURNAL BELONGS TO:

_____

&

_____

ONE
Question
A DAY
FOR
You & Me

Castle Point Books
New York

Enjoy answering these journal questions with someone you love. Enter the current year in the space provided and read the prompt. Jot down your answer on the gold lines and have your partner write his or her answer on the black lines. Enjoy sharing and comparing your responses as you get to know each other better!

ONE QUESTION A DAY FOR YOU & ME.
Copyright © 2018 by St. Martin's Press.

All rights reserved. Printed in Turkey.

For information, address St. Martin's Press,
175 Fifth Avenue, New York, N.Y. 10010.

www.castlepointbooks.com
www.stmartins.com

The Castle Point Books trademark is owned by Castle Point Publications, LLC.
Castle Point books are published and distributed by St. Martin's Press.

ISBN 978-1-250-16343-1 (trade paperback)

Our books may be purchased in bulk for promotional, educational, or business use.
Please contact your local bookseller or the Macmillan Corporate and
Premium Sales Department at 1-800-221-7945, extension 5442,
or by e-mail at MacmillanSpecialMarkets@macmillan.com.

First Edition: January 2018

10 9 8

January 1

What are your hopes for
the New Year?

Year: _____

_____

_____

_____

_____

Year: _____

_____

_____

_____

_____

Year: _____

_____

_____

_____

_____

January 2

What can you, as a couple, do better this year?

Year: _____

_____

_____

_____

_____

Year: _____

_____

_____

_____

_____

Year: _____

_____

_____

_____

_____

January 3

If you could change one thing in your
daily routine, what would it be?

Year: _____

_____

_____

_____

_____

Year: _____

_____

_____

_____

_____

Year: _____

_____

_____

_____

_____

January 4

If you could give one household chore
to your partner, what would it be?

Year: _____

_____

_____

_____

_____

Year: _____

_____

_____

_____

_____

Year: _____

_____

_____

_____

_____

January 5

What makes you feel loved?

Year: _____

_____

_____

_____

_____

Year: _____

_____

_____

_____

_____

Year: _____

_____

_____

_____

_____

January 6

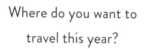

Where do you want to
travel this year?

Year: _____

_____

_____

_____

_____

Year: _____

_____

_____

_____

_____

Year: _____

_____

_____

_____

_____

January 7

If you could wake up anywhere tomorrow,
where would you want to be?

Year: _____

_____

_____

_____

_____

Year: _____

_____

_____

_____

_____

Year: _____

_____

_____

_____

_____

January 8

Who is the person you envy most?

Year: _____

_____

_____

_____

_____

Year: _____

_____

_____

_____

_____

Year: _____

_____

_____

_____

_____

January 9

What is one thing you would
change about your day?

Year: _____

_____

_____

_____

Year: _____

_____

_____

_____

Year: _____

_____

_____

_____

January 10

What event or milestone are you
most looking forward to?

Year: _____

_____

_____

_____

_____

Year: _____

_____

_____

_____

_____

Year: _____

_____

_____

_____

_____

January 11

What is the best news you've heard lately?

Year: _____

_____

_____

_____

_____

Year: _____

_____

_____

_____

_____

Year: _____

_____

_____

_____

_____

January 12

What is the last thing you got for free?

Year: _____

_____

_____

_____

_____

Year: _____

_____

_____

_____

_____

Year: _____

_____

_____

_____

_____

January 13

What makes you excited?

Year: _____

_____

_____

_____

_____

Year: _____

_____

_____

_____

_____

Year: _____

_____

_____

_____

_____

January 14

If you could change your career, what
would you do for work?

Year: _____

_____
_____
_____
_____

Year: _____

_____
_____
_____
_____

Year: _____

_____
_____
_____
_____

January 15

Do you believe in soulmates?

Year: _____

_____

_____

_____

_____

Year: _____

_____

_____

_____

_____

Year: _____

_____

_____

_____

_____

January 16

When I spend time alone,

I feel _____.

Year: _____

_____

_____

_____

_____

Year: _____

_____

_____

_____

_____

Year: _____

_____

_____

_____

_____

January 17

The most spontaneous thing

I've done is _____.

Year: _____

_____

_____

_____

_____

Year: _____

_____

_____

_____

_____

Year: _____

_____

_____

_____

_____

January 18

What can't you live without?

Year: _____

_____

_____

_____

_____

Year: _____

_____

_____

_____

_____

Year: _____

_____

_____

_____

_____

January 19

What natural talents do
you and your partner share?

Year: _____

_____

_____

_____

_____

Year: _____

_____

_____

_____

_____

Year: _____

_____

_____

_____

_____

January 20

When I come home to my partner,

I feel _____.

Year: _____

Year: _____

Year: _____

January 21

I wanted to tell my partner this
all day today: _____.

Year: _____

_____

_____

_____

_____

Year: _____

_____

_____

_____

_____

Year: _____

_____

_____

_____

_____

January 22

I worry about _____.

Year: _____

_____

_____

_____

_____

Year: _____

_____

_____

_____

_____

Year: _____

_____

_____

_____

_____

January 23

If you could change one thing about your
relationship, what would it be?

Year: _____

_____

_____

_____

_____

Year: _____

_____

_____

_____

_____

Year: _____

_____

_____

_____

_____

January 24

What are you most sensitive about?

Year: _____

_____

_____

_____

_____

Year: _____

_____

_____

_____

_____

Year: _____

_____

_____

_____

_____

January 25

It makes me happy when my partner

_____.

Year: _____

_____

_____

_____

_____

Year: _____

_____

_____

_____

_____

Year: _____

_____

_____

_____

_____

January 26

How sentimental are you?

Year: _____

_____

_____

_____

_____

Year: _____

_____

_____

_____

_____

Year: _____

_____

_____

_____

_____

January 27

What do you need to get rid of?

Year: _____

_____

_____

_____

_____

Year: _____

_____

_____

_____

_____

Year: _____

_____

_____

_____

_____

January 28

I feel giddy when _____.

Year: _____

_____

_____

_____

_____

Year: _____

_____

_____

_____

_____

Year: _____

_____

_____

_____

_____

January 29

What movie could you watch
over and over again?

Year: _____

_____

_____

_____

_____

Year: _____

_____

_____

_____

_____

Year: _____

_____

_____

_____

_____

January 30

When was the last time
your partner appeared in your dream?

Year: _____

_____

_____

_____

_____

Year: _____

_____

_____

_____

_____

Year: _____

_____

_____

_____

_____

January 31

If you could do any activity with your
partner, what would it be?

Year: _____

_____

_____

_____

_____

Year: _____

_____

_____

_____

_____

Year: _____

_____

_____

_____

_____

February 1

What part of your body
do you like the most?

Year: _____

_____

_____

_____

Year: _____

_____

_____

_____

Year: _____

_____

_____

_____

February 2

What gets you through a tough day?

Year: _____

_____

_____

_____

_____

Year: _____

_____

_____

_____

_____

Year: _____

_____

_____

_____

_____

February 3

What song makes you think of your partner?

Year: _____

_____

_____

_____

_____

Year: _____

_____

_____

_____

_____

Year: _____

_____

_____

_____

_____

February 4

If I were a poet, I'd compare my
partner to a _____ .

Year: _____

_____

_____

_____

Year: _____

_____

_____

_____

Year: _____

_____

_____

_____

February 5

What makes your heart race?

Year: _____

_____

_____

_____

Year: _____

_____

_____

_____

Year: _____

_____

_____

_____

February 6

What new friends have you made lately?

Year: _____

_____

_____

_____

Year: _____

_____

_____

_____

Year: _____

_____

_____

_____

February 7

Describe your dream home.

Year: _____

_____
_____
_____
_____

Year: _____

_____
_____
_____
_____

Year: _____

_____
_____
_____
_____

February 8

What experience would you
want to relive if you could?

Year: _____

_____

_____

_____

_____

Year: _____

_____

_____

_____

_____

Year: _____

_____

_____

_____

_____

February 9

What is the most dangerous
thing you've done lately?

Year: _____

_____

_____

_____

_____

Year: _____

_____

_____

_____

_____

Year: _____

_____

_____

_____

_____

February 10

Where do you go to think?

Year: _____

_____

_____

_____

Year: _____

_____

_____

_____

Year: _____

_____

_____

_____

February 11

One secret I know about my partner is:

_____.

Year: _____

_____

_____

_____

_____

Year: _____

_____

_____

_____

_____

Year: _____

_____

_____

_____

_____

February 12

What is your favorite color?

Year: _____

_____

_____

_____

_____

Year: _____

_____

_____

_____

_____

Year: _____

_____

_____

_____

_____

February 13

I like to brag about the fact that
my partner _____.

Year: _____

_____
_____
_____
_____

Year: _____

_____
_____
_____
_____

Year: _____

_____
_____
_____
_____

February 14

My partner means a lot to me because

_____.

Year: _____

_____

_____

_____

Year: _____

_____

_____

_____

Year: _____

_____

_____

_____

February 15

How often do you exercise?

Year: _____

_____

_____

_____

_____

Year: _____

_____

_____

_____

_____

Year: _____

_____

_____

_____

_____

February 16

My favorite meal to make is

_____.

Year: _____

_____
_____
_____
_____

Year: _____

_____
_____
_____
_____

Year: _____

_____
_____
_____
_____

February 17

Our last date was _____.

Year: _____

_____
_____
_____
_____

Year: _____

_____
_____
_____
_____

Year: _____

_____
_____
_____
_____

February 18

Our favorite date restaurant is

_____.

Year: _____

_____

_____

_____

_____

Year: _____

_____

_____

_____

_____

Year: _____

_____

_____

_____

_____

February 19

I get annoyed when _____.

Year: _____

_____
_____
_____
_____

Year: _____

_____
_____
_____
_____

Year: _____

_____
_____
_____
_____

February 20

My favorite thing about our relationship is

_____.

Year: _____

_____

_____

_____

_____

Year: _____

_____

_____

_____

_____

Year: _____

_____

_____

_____

_____

February 21

My favorite weather is _____.

Year: _____

_____
_____
_____
_____

Year: _____

_____
_____
_____
_____

Year: _____

_____
_____
_____
_____

February 22

What have you learned about yourself lately?

Year: _____

_____

_____

_____

Year: _____

_____

_____

_____

Year: _____

_____

_____

_____

February 23

What makes you feel defeated?

Year: _____

_____

_____

_____

_____

Year: _____

_____

_____

_____

_____

Year: _____

_____

_____

_____

_____

February 24

What was the last thing you won?

Year: _____

_____

_____

_____

_____

Year: _____

_____

_____

_____

_____

Year: _____

_____

_____

_____

_____

February 25

What did you eat for breakfast today?

Year: _____

_____

_____

_____

_____

Year: _____

_____

_____

_____

_____

Year: _____

_____

_____

_____

_____

February 26

I enjoy this about my partner:

_____.

Year: _____

_____

_____

_____

_____

Year: _____

_____

_____

_____

_____

Year: _____

_____

_____

_____

_____

February 27

What book have you read lately?

Year: _____

_____
_____
_____
_____

Year: _____

_____
_____
_____
_____

Year: _____

_____
_____
_____
_____

February 28

I like to tease my partner about

_____.

Year: _____

_____
_____
_____
_____

Year: _____

_____
_____
_____
_____

Year: _____

_____
_____
_____
_____

February 29

If I were deserted on an island with my partner,
the first thing I would do is _____.

Year: _____

_____

_____

_____

_____

Year: _____

_____

_____

_____

_____

Year: _____

_____

_____

_____

_____

March 1

What is your idea of a great evening out?

Year: _____

_____

_____

_____

_____

Year: _____

_____

_____

_____

_____

Year: _____

_____

_____

_____

_____

March 2

What are you saving for?

Year: _____

_____
_____
_____
_____

Year: _____

_____
_____
_____
_____

Year: _____

_____
_____
_____
_____

March 3

What drives you to be better?

Year: _____

_____

_____

_____

Year: _____

_____

_____

_____

Year: _____

_____

_____

_____

March 4

If you could change one thing about your
partner, what would you change?

Year: _____

_____

_____

_____

_____

Year: _____

_____

_____

_____

_____

Year: _____

_____

_____

_____

_____

March 5

What do you do when you're nervous?

Year: _____

_____

_____

_____

_____

Year: _____

_____

_____

_____

_____

Year: _____

_____

_____

_____

_____

March 6

For whom would you do anything, and why?

Year: _____

_____

_____

_____

_____

Year: _____

_____

_____

_____

_____

Year: _____

_____

_____

_____

_____

March 7

My favorite sport to watch with my
partner is _____.

Year: _____

_____

_____

_____

Year: _____

_____

_____

_____

Year: _____

_____

_____

_____

March 8

What nickname or pet name
do you like being called?

Year: _____

_____

_____

_____

Year: _____

_____

_____

_____

Year: _____

_____

_____

_____

March 9

What attracts you to your partner?

Year: _____

_____

_____

_____

Year: _____

_____

_____

_____

Year: _____

_____

_____

_____

March 10

Before I fall asleep, I like to _____.

Year: _____

_____

_____

_____

Year: _____

_____

_____

_____

Year: _____

_____

_____

_____

March 11

What plan on your calendar would you
cancel if you could?

Year: _____

_____

_____

_____

_____

Year: _____

_____

_____

_____

_____

Year: _____

_____

_____

_____

_____

March 12

I need my partner's support when I

_____.

Year: _____

_____

_____

_____

_____

Year: _____

_____

_____

_____

_____

Year: _____

_____

_____

_____

_____

March 13

I hate having to _____.

Year: _____

_____
_____
_____
_____

Year: _____

_____
_____
_____
_____

Year: _____

_____
_____
_____
_____

March 14

Happiness is being _____.

Year: _____

_____

_____

_____

_____

Year: _____

_____

_____

_____

_____

Year: _____

_____

_____

_____

_____

March 15

What thoughts do you
share only with your partner?

Year: _____

_____

_____

_____

Year: _____

_____

_____

_____

Year: _____

_____

_____

_____

March 16

What is one thing you like
to do for your partner?

Year: _____

_____
_____
_____
_____

Year: _____

_____
_____
_____
_____

Year: _____

_____
_____
_____
_____

March 17

I am most peaceful when _____.

Year: _____

_____

_____

_____

_____

Year: _____

_____

_____

_____

_____

Year: _____

_____

_____

_____

_____

March 18

How independent are you?

Year: _____

_____
_____
_____
_____

Year: _____

_____
_____
_____
_____

Year: _____

_____
_____
_____
_____

March 19

Three words I'd use to describe my

partner are _____.

Year: _____

_____

_____

_____

_____

Year: _____

_____

_____

_____

_____

Year: _____

_____

_____

_____

_____

March 20

When I am outside, I love to

_____.

Year: _____

_____

_____

_____

_____

Year: _____

_____

_____

_____

_____

Year: _____

_____

_____

_____

_____

March 21

If I could fly anywhere with my partner,
I would fly to _____.

Year: _____

_____
_____
_____
_____

Year: _____

_____
_____
_____
_____

Year: _____

_____
_____
_____
_____

March 22

Where would you live
if you could live anywhere?

Year: _____

_____

_____

_____

_____

Year: _____

_____

_____

_____

_____

Year: _____

_____

_____

_____

_____

March 23

What have you learned
from your parents' marriage?

Year: _____

_____

_____

_____

Year: _____

_____

_____

_____

Year: _____

_____

_____

_____

March 24

What bothered you today?

Year: _____

_____

_____

_____

_____

Year: _____

_____

_____

_____

_____

Year: _____

_____

_____

_____

_____

March 25

I last cried about _____.

Year: _____

_____

_____

_____

_____

Year: _____

_____

_____

_____

_____

Year: _____

_____

_____

_____

_____

March 26

What makes you feel like a kid?

Year: _____

_____
_____
_____
_____

Year: _____

_____
_____
_____
_____

Year: _____

_____
_____
_____
_____

March 27

My favorite flower is _____.

Year: _____

_____

_____

_____

_____

Year: _____

_____

_____

_____

_____

Year: _____

_____

_____

_____

_____

March 28

I love when my partner surprises me with

_____.

Year: _____

_____

_____

_____

_____

Year: _____

_____

_____

_____

_____

Year: _____

_____

_____

_____

_____

March 29

What friend of your partner's
is your least favorite?

Year: _____

Year: _____

Year: _____

March 30

Truth or Dare?

Year: _____

_____

_____

_____

_____

Year: _____

_____

_____

_____

_____

Year: _____

_____

_____

_____

_____

March 31

Our guilty pleasures are _____.

Year: _____

_____

_____

_____

_____

Year: _____

_____

_____

_____

_____

Year: _____

_____

_____

_____

_____

April 1

How many times have you thought about
kissing your partner today?

Year: _____

Year: _____

Year: _____

April 2

When my partner looks at me, I feel

_____.

Year: _____

_____

_____

_____

Year: _____

_____

_____

_____

Year: _____

_____

_____

_____

April 3

If I wrote a story about my partner, the
first sentence would be _____.

Year: _____

_____

_____

_____

_____

Year: _____

_____

_____

_____

Year: _____

_____

_____

_____

_____

April 4

What comforts you?

Year: _____

_____

_____

_____

Year: _____

_____

_____

_____

Year: _____

_____

_____

_____

April 5

One of our best memories together is

_____.

Year: _____

_____

_____

_____

_____

Year: _____

_____

_____

_____

_____

Year: _____

_____

_____

_____

_____

April 6

If you could buy a new car, what would it be?

Year: _____

_____

_____

_____

_____

Year: _____

_____

_____

_____

_____

Year: _____

_____

_____

_____

_____

April 7

What have you told your
closest friend about your partner?

Year: _____

_____

_____

_____

_____

Year: _____

_____

_____

_____

_____

Year: _____

_____

_____

_____

_____

April 8

Which of your partner's
friends do you like best?

Year: _____

_____

_____

_____

Year: _____

_____

_____

_____

Year: _____

_____

_____

_____

April 9

_____ makes me want

to be a better person.

Year: _____

_____

_____

_____

Year: _____

_____

_____

_____

Year: _____

_____

_____

_____

April 10

One thing I'd like to change about myself
is _____.

Year: _____

_____

_____

_____

_____

Year: _____

_____

_____

_____

_____

Year: _____

_____

_____

_____

_____

April 11

What is your usual breakfast?

Year: _____

_____

_____

_____

Year: _____

_____

_____

_____

Year: _____

_____

_____

_____

April 12

How happy are you?

Year: _____

_____

_____

_____

_____

Year: _____

_____

_____

_____

_____

Year: _____

_____

_____

_____

April 13

What is your favorite store?

Year: _____

_____

_____

_____

Year: _____

_____

_____

_____

Year: _____

_____

_____

_____

April 14

What website did you last visit?

Year: ————

_____

_____

_____

_____

Year: ————

_____

_____

_____

_____

Year: ————

_____

_____

_____

_____

April 15

What do you cook most often?

Year: _____

_____

_____

_____

_____

Year: _____

_____

_____

_____

_____

Year: _____

_____

_____

_____

_____

April 16

What superstitions do you have?

Year: _____

_____

_____

_____

_____

Year: _____

_____

_____

_____

_____

Year: _____

_____

_____

_____

_____

April 17

If you could do one thing with your partner
for 30 minutes, what would you do?

Year: _____

_____

_____

_____

_____

Year: _____

_____

_____

_____

_____

Year: _____

_____

_____

_____

_____

April 18

What do you daydream about?

Year: _____

_____

_____

_____

_____

Year: _____

_____

_____

_____

_____

Year: _____

_____

_____

_____

_____

April 19

How fun are you at a party?

Year: _____

_____
_____
_____
_____

Year: _____

_____
_____
_____
_____

Year: _____

_____
_____
_____
_____

April 20

What is your favorite part of your job?

Year: _____

_____

_____

_____

Year: _____

_____

_____

_____

Year: _____

_____

_____

_____

April 21

Our home is a home because

_____.

Year: _____

_____

_____

_____

_____

Year: _____

_____

_____

_____

_____

Year: _____

_____

_____

_____

_____

April 22

Do you think of yourself as laid back, extra
motivated, or somewhere in the middle?

Year: _____

_____

_____

_____

Year: _____

_____

_____

_____

Year: _____

_____

_____

_____

April 23

What do you hope never changes about
your partner?

Year: _____

_____
_____
_____
_____

Year: _____

_____
_____
_____
_____

Year: _____

_____
_____
_____
_____

April 24

If you called in sick, what would you do
with your day?

Year: _____

_____

_____

_____

_____

Year: _____

_____

_____

_____

_____

Year: _____

_____

_____

_____

_____

April 25

What is the last television series you
enjoyed watching together?

Year: _____

_____

_____

_____

_____

Year: _____

_____

_____

_____

_____

Year: _____

_____

_____

_____

_____

April 26

I love it when my partner wears

_____.

Year: _____

_____

_____

_____

_____

Year: _____

_____

_____

_____

_____

Year: _____

_____

_____

_____

_____

April 27

Who is your mentor?

Year: _____

_____
_____
_____
_____

Year: _____

_____
_____
_____
_____

Year: _____

_____
_____
_____
_____

April 28

Would you want to live forever? Why?

Year: _____

_____
_____
_____
_____

Year: _____

_____
_____
_____
_____

Year: _____

_____
_____
_____
_____

April 29

If you could relive one moment in your relationship, which moment would you choose?

Year: _____

_____

_____

_____

_____

Year: _____

_____

_____

_____

_____

Year: _____

_____

_____

_____

_____

April 30

Who have you talked to the most today?

Year: _____

_____

_____

_____

_____

Year: _____

_____

_____

_____

_____

Year: _____

_____

_____

_____

_____

May 1

How do you like to celebrate your birthday?

Year: _____

_____

_____

_____

Year: _____

_____

_____

_____

Year: _____

_____

_____

_____

May 2

The best part of my partner's body is

_____ .

Year: _____

_____
_____
_____
_____

Year: _____

_____
_____
_____
_____

Year: _____

_____
_____
_____
_____

May 3

Who needs you more than you need them?

Year: _____

_____
_____
_____
_____

Year: _____

_____
_____
_____
_____

Year: _____

_____
_____
_____
_____

May 4

What was the last thing you
bought together?

Year: _____

_____

_____

_____

Year: _____

_____

_____

_____

Year: _____

_____

_____

_____

May 5

What are you sensitive about right now?

Year: _____

_____

_____

_____

Year: _____

_____

_____

_____

Year: _____

_____

_____

_____

May 6

If you could have one wish granted,
what would it be?

Year: _____

_____
_____
_____
_____

Year: _____

_____
_____
_____
_____

Year: _____

_____
_____
_____
_____

May 7

Which colors look best on you?

Year: _____

_____
_____
_____

Year: _____

_____
_____
_____

Year: _____

_____
_____
_____

May 8

What romantic gesture would
you like your partner to make?

Year: _____

_____

_____

_____

Year: _____

_____

_____

_____

Year: _____

_____

_____

_____

May 9

If I could go to any concert,

it would be _____.

Year: _____

_____

_____

_____

_____

Year: _____

_____

_____

_____

_____

Year: _____

_____

_____

_____

_____

May 10

If you could do anything today,
what would it be?

Year: _____

_____
_____
_____
_____

Year: _____

_____
_____
_____
_____

Year: _____

_____
_____
_____
_____

May 11

The most recent development in our
relationship was _____.

Year: _____

_____
_____
_____
_____

Year: _____

_____
_____
_____
_____

Year: _____

_____
_____
_____
_____

May 12

If you were to give your partner an award,
what would it be for?

Year: _____

_____

_____

_____

_____

Year: _____

_____

_____

_____

_____

Year: _____

_____

_____

_____

_____

May 13

What is mind-blowing right now?

Year: _____

_____

_____

_____

_____

Year: _____

_____

_____

_____

_____

Year: _____

_____

_____

_____

_____

May 14

If you were to start a business together,
what would it be?

Year: _____

_____

_____

_____

_____

Year: _____

_____

_____

_____

_____

Year: _____

_____

_____

_____

_____

May 15

If you could play a sport together,
what would it be?

Year: _____

_____
_____
_____
_____

Year: _____

_____
_____
_____
_____

Year: _____

_____
_____
_____
_____

May 16

What is ahead of you?

Year: _____

_____

_____

_____

_____

Year: _____

_____

_____

_____

_____

Year: _____

_____

_____

_____

_____

May 17

What is your favorite food?

Year: _____

_____

_____

_____

Year: _____

_____

_____

_____

Year: _____

_____

_____

_____

May 18

What celebrity does your
partner resemble?

Year: _____

_____

_____

_____

_____

Year: _____

_____

_____

_____

_____

Year: _____

_____

_____

_____

May 19

What holiday do you love, and why?

Year: _____

_____
_____
_____
_____

Year: _____

_____
_____
_____
_____

Year: _____

_____
_____
_____
_____

May 20

If you could be a wild animal,

what would you be?

Year: _____

_____

_____

_____

_____

Year: _____

_____

_____

_____

_____

Year: _____

_____

_____

_____

_____

May 21

Do you think your partner is romantic,
and if so, how?

Year: _____

_____

_____

_____

_____

Year: _____

_____

_____

_____

_____

Year: _____

_____

_____

_____

_____

May 22

Do you have a budget,
and if so, do you follow it?

Year: _____

_____

_____

_____

_____

Year: _____

_____

_____

_____

_____

Year: _____

_____

_____

_____

_____

May 23

What made you laugh today?

Year: _____

_____

_____

_____

_____

Year: _____

_____

_____

_____

_____

Year: _____

_____

_____

_____

_____

May 24

If you could pick a theme song for your
relationship, what would it be?

Year: _____

Year: _____

Year: _____

May 25

On what topic do you feel like an expert?

Year: _____

_____

_____

_____

_____

Year: _____

_____

_____

_____

_____

Year: _____

_____

_____

_____

_____

May 26

My partner makes me laugh when he/she

_____.

Year: _____

_____
_____
_____
_____

Year: _____

_____
_____
_____
_____

Year: _____

_____
_____
_____
_____

May 27

Who in your life is most like you?

Year: _____

_____

_____

_____

_____

Year: _____

_____

_____

_____

_____

Year: _____

_____

_____

_____

_____

May 28

How many times did you
think about sex today?

Year: _____

_____

_____

_____

Year: _____

_____

_____

_____

Year: _____

_____

_____

_____

May 29

What problem would you like to escape?

Year: _____

_____
_____
_____
_____

Year: _____

_____
_____
_____
_____

Year: _____

_____
_____
_____
_____

May 30

What do you enjoy most
about having people over?

Year: _____

_____
_____
_____
_____

Year: _____

_____
_____
_____
_____

Year: _____

_____
_____
_____
_____

May 31

What would you include in a
time capsule of your relationship?

Year: _____

_____

_____

_____

_____

Year: _____

_____

_____

_____

_____

Year: _____

_____

_____

_____

_____

June 1

If you had a million dollars,
how would you spend it?

Year: _____

_____

_____

_____

Year: _____

_____

_____

_____

Year: _____

_____

_____

_____

June 2

What is the last thing you
want to do today?

Year: _____

_____

_____

_____

_____

Year: _____

_____

_____

_____

_____

Year: _____

_____

_____

_____

_____

June 3

I am scared of _____.

Year: _____

_____

_____

_____

Year: _____

_____

_____

_____

Year: _____

_____

_____

_____

June 4

Loving you is _____.

Year: _____

_____
_____
_____
_____

Year: _____

_____
_____
_____
_____

Year: _____

_____
_____
_____
_____

June 5

The foundation of our relationship is

_____.

Year: _____

_____

_____

_____

_____

Year: _____

_____

_____

_____

_____

Year: _____

_____

_____

_____

_____

June 6

What animal would be your perfect pet?

Year: _____

_____
_____
_____
_____

Year: _____

_____
_____
_____
_____

Year: _____

_____
_____
_____
_____

June 7

What is your partner's most attractive quality?

Year: _____

_____

_____

_____

_____

Year: _____

_____

_____

_____

_____

Year: _____

_____

_____

_____

_____

June 8

Six months from now, where
do you see yourselves?

Year: _____

_____

_____

_____

_____

Year: _____

_____

_____

_____

_____

Year: _____

_____

_____

_____

_____

June 9

I appreciate it when my partner

_____.

Year: _____

_____

_____

_____

_____

Year: _____

_____

_____

_____

_____

Year: _____

_____

_____

_____

_____

June 10

Where is your favorite
place to go to breakfast?

Year: _____

_____
_____
_____
_____

Year: _____

_____
_____
_____
_____

Year: _____

_____
_____
_____
_____

June 11

Today was special because _____.

Year: _____

_____
_____
_____

Year: _____

_____
_____
_____

Year: _____

_____
_____
_____

June 12

When I kiss my partner, I feel

_____.

Year: _____

_____
_____
_____
_____

Year: _____

_____
_____
_____
_____

Year: _____

_____
_____
_____
_____

June 13

I'm at my best when I'm _____.

Year: _____

_____

_____

_____

_____

Year: _____

_____

_____

_____

_____

Year: _____

_____

_____

_____

_____

June 14

Don't talk to me when I'm _____.

Year: _____

_____
_____
_____
_____

Year: _____

_____
_____
_____
_____

Year: _____

_____
_____
_____
_____

June 15

I find myself distracted by

_____.

Year: _____

_____

_____

_____

_____

Year: _____

_____

_____

_____

_____

Year: _____

_____

_____

_____

_____

June 16

My partner helps me with

_____.

Year: _____

_____

_____

_____

_____

Year: _____

_____

_____

_____

_____

Year: _____

_____

_____

_____

_____

June 17

Before I met my partner, I was

_____ .

Year: _____

_____

_____

_____

Year: _____

_____

_____

_____

Year: _____

_____

_____

_____

June 18

My partner and I will have a happy story
because _____.

Year: _____

_____

_____

_____

Year: _____

_____

_____

_____

Year: _____

_____

_____

_____

June 19

If you could take your partner back to your childhood town, what would you show him/her?

Year: _____

_____

_____

_____

Year: _____

_____

_____

_____

Year: _____

_____

_____

_____

June 20

What's the saddest thing
that has ever happened to you?

Year: _____

_____

_____

_____

Year: _____

_____

_____

_____

Year: _____

_____

_____

_____

June 21

I make my partner laugh when I

_____.

Year: _____

_____

_____

_____

_____

Year: _____

_____

_____

_____

_____

Year: _____

_____

_____

_____

_____

June 22

When I look at my partner from across
the room, I feel _____.

Year: _____

_____
_____
_____
_____

Year: _____

_____
_____
_____
_____

Year: _____

_____
_____
_____
_____

June 23

My parents' favorite thing about my
partner is _____.

Year: _____

_____
_____
_____

Year: _____

_____
_____
_____

Year: _____

_____
_____
_____

June 24

The most outrageous text I've sent my

partner was _____.

Year: _____
_____
_____
_____
_____

Year: _____
_____
_____
_____
_____

Year: _____
_____
_____
_____
_____

June 25

What required patience today?

Year: _____

_____

_____

_____

Year: _____

_____

_____

_____

Year: _____

_____

_____

_____

June 26

When was the last time you got in trouble?

Year: _____

_____
_____
_____
_____

Year: _____

_____
_____
_____
_____

Year: _____

_____
_____
_____
_____

June 27

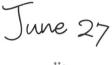

What is something you are glad
to never have to do again?

Year: _____

_____

_____

_____

Year: _____

_____

_____

_____

Year: _____

_____

_____

_____

June 28

What task do you put off until the last minute?

Year: _____

_____

_____

_____

Year: _____

_____

_____

_____

Year: _____

_____

_____

_____

June 29

What is the best thing you
bring to your relationship?

Year: _____

_____

_____

_____

Year: _____

_____

_____

_____

Year: _____

_____

_____

_____

June 30

What is something you consider
absolutely unforgivable?

Year: _____

_____

_____

_____

_____

Year: _____

_____

_____

_____

_____

Year: _____

_____

_____

_____

_____

July 1

If you had no fear,
what would you dare to do?

Year: _____

_____

_____

_____

Year: _____

_____

_____

_____

Year: _____

_____

_____

_____

July 2

What is the biggest
blessing in your life?

Year: _____

_____

_____

_____

_____

Year: _____

_____

_____

_____

_____

Year: _____

_____

_____

_____

_____

July 3

What behavior can you not tolerate?

Year: _____

_____

_____

_____

Year: _____

_____

_____

_____

Year: _____

_____

_____

_____

July 4

If you could use three words to describe
your younger self, what would they be?

Year: _____

_____

_____

_____

_____

Year: _____

_____

_____

_____

_____

Year: _____

_____

_____

_____

_____

July 5

Do you follow your head or heart
when making decisions?

Year: _____

_____

_____

_____

_____

Year: _____

_____

_____

_____

_____

Year: _____

_____

_____

_____

_____

July 6

What is your favorite book?

Year: _____

_____

_____

_____

Year: _____

_____

_____

_____

Year: _____

_____

_____

_____

July 7

What is something that never ends well?

Year: _____

_____
_____
_____
_____

Year: _____

_____
_____
_____
_____

Year: _____

_____
_____
_____
_____

July 8

What is your your favorite
word or saying?

Year: _____

_____

_____

_____

_____

Year: _____

_____

_____

_____

_____

Year: _____

_____

_____

_____

_____

July 9

Which do you like more: kissing or hugging?

Year: _____

_____

_____

_____

_____

Year: _____

_____

_____

_____

_____

Year: _____

_____

_____

_____

_____

July 10

What aspect of your
relationship needs work?

Year: _____

_____

_____

_____

_____

Year: _____

_____

_____

_____

_____

Year: _____

_____

_____

_____

_____

July 11

How do you like being taken care of
when you're sick?

Year: _____

_____
_____
_____
_____

Year: _____

_____
_____
_____
_____

Year: _____

_____
_____
_____
_____

July 12

What class do you think you would
enjoy taking together?

Year: _____

_____

_____

_____

_____

Year: _____

_____

_____

_____

_____

Year: _____

_____

_____

_____

_____

July 13

What is the best thing
your partner has done for you?

Year: _____

_____

_____

_____

Year: _____

_____

_____

_____

Year: _____

_____

_____

_____

July 14

What are your relationship deal breakers?

Year: _____

_____

_____

_____

_____

Year: _____

_____

_____

_____

_____

Year: _____

_____

_____

_____

_____

July 15

Do you fantasize about your partner
during the day, and if so, in what way?

Year: _____

_____

_____

_____

Year: _____

_____

_____

_____

Year: _____

_____

_____

_____

July 16

What was your favorite movie this year?

Year: _____

_____

_____

_____

_____

Year: _____

_____

_____

_____

_____

Year: _____

_____

_____

_____

_____

July 17

What do you want to do when you retire?

Year: _____

_____

_____

_____

Year: _____

_____

_____

_____

Year: _____

_____

_____

_____

July 18

Who has recently taught you a life lesson?

Year: _____

_____

_____

_____

Year: _____

_____

_____

_____

Year: _____

_____

_____

_____

July 19

Where do you want to take a road trip?

Year: _____

_____

_____

_____

_____

Year: _____

_____

_____

_____

_____

Year: _____

_____

_____

_____

_____

July 20

Describe a time in the last week
when you were angry.

Year: _____

_____

_____

_____

Year: _____

_____

_____

_____

Year: _____

_____

_____

_____

July 21

Which of your physical traits
would you change if you could?

Year: _____

_____

_____

_____

Year: _____

_____

_____

_____

Year: _____

_____

_____

_____

July 22

What is the first childhood memory
that comes to mind right now?

Year: _____

_____

_____

_____

_____

Year: _____

_____

_____

_____

_____

Year: _____

_____

_____

_____

_____

July 23

Where do you want to live
in the next 10 years?

Year: _____

_____

_____

_____

Year: _____

_____

_____

_____

Year: _____

_____

_____

_____

July 24

What would you like best: a year off to
travel, a vacation house, or a boat?

Year: _____

_____
_____
_____
_____

Year: _____

_____
_____
_____
_____

Year: _____

_____
_____
_____
_____

July 25

What would you do with an extra $100
a month to spend on yourself?

Year: _____

_____

_____

_____

_____

Year: _____

_____

_____

_____

_____

Year: _____

_____

_____

_____

_____

July 26

What makes your partner different from
other lovers you've had in the past?

Year: _____

_____

_____

_____

_____

Year: _____

_____

_____

_____

_____

Year: _____

_____

_____

_____

_____

July 27

Of what are you most proud?

Year: _____

_____

_____

_____

Year: _____

_____

_____

_____

Year: _____

_____

_____

_____

July 28

If you had to guess,
what is your partner thinking right now?

Year: ⎯⎯⎯⎯

⎯⎯⎯⎯⎯⎯⎯⎯⎯⎯⎯⎯⎯⎯⎯⎯⎯⎯⎯⎯⎯⎯⎯⎯⎯⎯⎯⎯⎯⎯⎯⎯

⎯⎯⎯⎯⎯⎯⎯⎯⎯⎯⎯⎯⎯⎯⎯⎯⎯⎯⎯⎯⎯⎯⎯⎯⎯⎯⎯⎯⎯⎯⎯⎯

⎯⎯⎯⎯⎯⎯⎯⎯⎯⎯⎯⎯⎯⎯⎯⎯⎯⎯⎯⎯⎯⎯⎯⎯⎯⎯⎯⎯⎯⎯⎯⎯

⎯⎯⎯⎯⎯⎯⎯⎯⎯⎯⎯⎯⎯⎯⎯⎯⎯⎯⎯⎯⎯⎯⎯⎯⎯⎯⎯⎯⎯⎯⎯⎯

Year: ⎯⎯⎯⎯

⎯⎯⎯⎯⎯⎯⎯⎯⎯⎯⎯⎯⎯⎯⎯⎯⎯⎯⎯⎯⎯⎯⎯⎯⎯⎯⎯⎯⎯⎯⎯⎯

⎯⎯⎯⎯⎯⎯⎯⎯⎯⎯⎯⎯⎯⎯⎯⎯⎯⎯⎯⎯⎯⎯⎯⎯⎯⎯⎯⎯⎯⎯⎯⎯

⎯⎯⎯⎯⎯⎯⎯⎯⎯⎯⎯⎯⎯⎯⎯⎯⎯⎯⎯⎯⎯⎯⎯⎯⎯⎯⎯⎯⎯⎯⎯⎯

⎯⎯⎯⎯⎯⎯⎯⎯⎯⎯⎯⎯⎯⎯⎯⎯⎯⎯⎯⎯⎯⎯⎯⎯⎯⎯⎯⎯⎯⎯⎯⎯

Year: ⎯⎯⎯⎯

⎯⎯⎯⎯⎯⎯⎯⎯⎯⎯⎯⎯⎯⎯⎯⎯⎯⎯⎯⎯⎯⎯⎯⎯⎯⎯⎯⎯⎯⎯⎯⎯

⎯⎯⎯⎯⎯⎯⎯⎯⎯⎯⎯⎯⎯⎯⎯⎯⎯⎯⎯⎯⎯⎯⎯⎯⎯⎯⎯⎯⎯⎯⎯⎯

⎯⎯⎯⎯⎯⎯⎯⎯⎯⎯⎯⎯⎯⎯⎯⎯⎯⎯⎯⎯⎯⎯⎯⎯⎯⎯⎯⎯⎯⎯⎯⎯

⎯⎯⎯⎯⎯⎯⎯⎯⎯⎯⎯⎯⎯⎯⎯⎯⎯⎯⎯⎯⎯⎯⎯⎯⎯⎯⎯⎯⎯⎯⎯⎯

July 29

What is the best thing
about your relationship?

Year: _____

_____

_____

_____

_____

Year: _____

_____

_____

_____

_____

Year: _____

_____

_____

_____

_____

July 30

What is the juiciest gossip
you have heard lately?

Year: _____

_____
_____
_____
_____

Year: _____

_____
_____
_____
_____

Year: _____

_____
_____
_____
_____

July 31

What is your biggest pet peeve?

Year: _____

_____

_____

_____

_____

Year: _____

_____

_____

_____

_____

Year: _____

_____

_____

_____

_____

August 1

What is the most lovable thing
about your partner?

Year: _____

_____

_____

_____

_____

Year: _____

_____

_____

_____

_____

Year: _____

_____

_____

_____

_____

August 2

What is one small thing you wish
your partner would do on a regular basis?

Year: _____

_____

_____

_____

Year: _____

_____

_____

_____

Year: _____

_____

_____

_____

August 3

What would you like to do
more as a couple?

Year: _____

_____

_____

_____

Year: _____

_____

_____

_____

Year: _____

_____

_____

_____

August 4

Describe one thing your partner does
that makes you feel loved.

Year: _____

_____
_____
_____
_____

Year: _____

_____
_____
_____
_____

Year: _____

_____
_____
_____
_____

August 5

What is one thing that you
secretly want to ask your partner?

Year: _____

_____

_____

_____

_____

Year: _____

_____

_____

_____

_____

Year: _____

_____

_____

_____

_____

August 6

When did you last tell your partner that
you loved him/her?

Year: _____

_____

_____

_____

Year: _____

_____

_____

_____

Year: _____

_____

_____

_____

August 7

What are your biggest strengths as a couple?

Year: _____

_____

_____

_____

Year: _____

_____

_____

_____

Year: _____

_____

_____

_____

August 8

How can you be a better partner?

Year: _____

Year: _____

Year: _____

August 9

What is your favorite snack?

Year: _____

_____

_____

_____

Year: _____

_____

_____

_____

Year: _____

_____

_____

_____

August 10

Is your career fulfilling? If not,
what would make it more fulfilling?

Year: _____

_____

_____

_____

Year: _____

_____

_____

_____

Year: _____

_____

_____

_____

August 11

What five things do you love
most about your partner?

Year: _____

_____

_____

_____

_____

Year: _____

_____

_____

_____

_____

Year: _____

_____

_____

_____

_____

August 12

Name something you are scared to try.

Year: _____

_____
_____
_____

Year: _____

_____
_____
_____

Year: _____

_____
_____
_____

August 13

What beautiful thing did you admire today?

Year: _____

_____
_____
_____
_____

Year: _____

_____
_____
_____
_____

Year: _____

_____
_____
_____
_____

August 14

Where do you go for answers?

Year: _____

_____

_____

_____

_____

Year: _____

_____

_____

_____

_____

Year: _____

_____

_____

_____

_____

August 15

Where did you go today?

Year: _____

_____
_____
_____
_____

Year: _____

_____
_____
_____
_____

Year: _____

_____
_____
_____
_____

August 16

If you could be someone famous,
who would you be?

Year: _____

_____

_____

_____

Year: _____

_____

_____

_____

Year: _____

_____

_____

_____

August 17

What are you searching for?

Year: _____

_____
_____
_____
_____

Year: _____

_____
_____
_____
_____

Year: _____

_____
_____
_____
_____

August 18

If you could play an instrument,
which one would you play?

Year: _____

_____

_____

_____

Year: _____

_____

_____

_____

Year: _____

_____

_____

_____

August 19

What song is at the top of your playlist?

Year: _____

_____

_____

_____

Year: _____

_____

_____

_____

Year: _____

_____

_____

_____

August 20

_____ is totally overrated.

Year: _____

_____

_____

_____

_____

Year: _____

_____

_____

_____

_____

Year: _____

_____

_____

_____

_____

August 21

Being around children makes me

_____.

Year: _____

_____

_____

_____

_____

Year: _____

_____

_____

_____

_____

Year: _____

_____

_____

_____

_____

August 22

When was the last time you annoyed or
upset your partner?

Year: _____

_____

_____

_____

Year: _____

_____

_____

_____

Year: _____

_____

_____

_____

August 23

What do you wish you were better at?

Year: _____

_____

_____

_____

_____

Year: _____

_____

_____

_____

_____

Year: _____

_____

_____

_____

_____

August 24

What was the biggest change in your life
in the last year?

Year: _____

_____

_____

_____

Year: _____

_____

_____

_____

Year: _____

_____

_____

_____

August 25

What puts you to sleep?

Year: _____

_____

_____

_____

_____

Year: _____

_____

_____

_____

_____

Year: _____

_____

_____

_____

_____

August 26

Who is more outgoing in your
relationship, and why do you think that?

Year: _____

_____

_____

_____

_____

Year: _____

_____

_____

_____

_____

Year: _____

_____

_____

_____

_____

August 27

What question would you like answered?

Year: _____

_____
_____
_____
_____

Year: _____

_____
_____
_____
_____

Year: _____

_____
_____
_____
_____

August 28

What activity do you wish
you did more often?

Year: _____

_____

_____

_____

Year: _____

_____

_____

_____

Year: _____

_____

_____

_____

August 29

What are your goals?

Year: _____

_____

_____

_____

_____

Year: _____

_____

_____

_____

_____

Year: _____

_____

_____

_____

_____

August 30

How do you have fun together?

Year: _____

_____

_____

_____

_____

Year: _____

_____

_____

_____

_____

Year: _____

_____

_____

_____

_____

August 31

What is happening in the lives
of your extended family?

Year: _____

_____

_____

_____

Year: _____

_____

_____

_____

Year: _____

_____

_____

_____

September 1

Where do you see yourself
in three years?

Year: _____

_____
_____
_____
_____

Year: _____

_____
_____
_____
_____

Year: _____

_____
_____
_____
_____

September 2

Who are your most supportive
friends/family members?

Year: _____

_____

_____

_____

_____

Year: _____

_____

_____

_____

_____

Year: _____

_____

_____

_____

_____

September 3

What friend/family relationship are you
working on right now?

Year: _____

_____

_____

_____

Year: _____

_____

_____

_____

Year: _____

_____

_____

_____

September 4

If you could get in your car and drive
anywhere today, where would you go?

Year: _____

_____

_____

_____

_____

Year: _____

_____

_____

_____

_____

Year: _____

_____

_____

_____

_____

September 5

What is the last thing you lost?

Year: _____

_____

_____

_____

Year: _____

_____

_____

_____

Year: _____

_____

_____

_____

September 6

What could you do to make your partner
feel more secure?

Year: _____

_____

_____

_____

_____

Year: _____

_____

_____

_____

_____

Year: _____

_____

_____

_____

_____

September 7

What did you learn this year
about your relationship?

Year: _____

_____

_____

_____

Year: _____

_____

_____

_____

Year: _____

_____

_____

_____

September 8

What is the worst thing that
happened to you this year?

Year: _____

_____

_____

_____

Year: _____

_____

_____

_____

Year: _____

_____

_____

_____

September 9

Who has disagreed with you lately?

Year: _____

_____

_____

_____

Year: _____

_____

_____

_____

Year: _____

_____

_____

_____

September 10

How well do you take care of yourself?

Year: _____

_____
_____
_____
_____

Year: _____

_____
_____
_____
_____

Year: _____

_____
_____
_____
_____

September 11

What brings you joy and satisfaction?

Year: _____

_____

_____

_____

_____

Year: _____

_____

_____

_____

_____

Year: _____

_____

_____

_____

_____

September 12

What are your strongest desires?

Year: _____

_____

_____

_____

Year: _____

_____

_____

_____

Year: _____

_____

_____

_____

September 13

How do you balance the need for
"we time" and "me time"?

Year: _____

_____

_____

_____

Year: _____

_____

_____

_____

Year: _____

_____

_____

_____

September 14

What's your idea of a romantic vacation?

Year: _____

_____

_____

_____

_____

Year: _____

_____

_____

_____

_____

Year: _____

_____

_____

_____

_____

September 15

What do you notice about your partner today?

Year: _____

_____
_____
_____
_____

Year: _____

_____
_____
_____
_____

Year: _____

_____
_____
_____
_____

September 16

What is one treasured memory
from this past year?

Year: _____

_____
_____
_____
_____

Year: _____

_____
_____
_____
_____

Year: _____

_____
_____
_____
_____

September 17

What word best describes your
relationship?

Year: _____

_____
_____
_____
_____

Year: _____

_____
_____
_____
_____

Year: _____

_____
_____
_____
_____

September 18

Which of your friends seems to have the
healthiest or happiest relationship?

Year: _____

_____

_____

_____

Year: _____

_____

_____

_____

Year: _____

_____

_____

_____

September 19

What is your wildest sexual fantasy?

Year: _____

_____

_____

_____

_____

Year: _____

_____

_____

_____

_____

Year: _____

_____

_____

_____

_____

September 20

What kind of parent do you want to be?

Year: _____

_____

_____

_____

Year: _____

_____

_____

_____

Year: _____

_____

_____

_____

September 21

What change can you make to be healthier?

Year: _____

_____

_____

_____

_____

Year: _____

_____

_____

_____

_____

Year: _____

_____

_____

_____

_____

September 22

How often is often enough
when it comes to sex?

Year: _____

_____

_____

_____

_____

Year: _____

_____

_____

_____

_____

Year: _____

_____

_____

_____

_____

September 23

If you had a year left to live,
what would you do with it?

Year: _____

_____

_____

_____

Year: _____

_____

_____

_____

Year: _____

_____

_____

_____

September 24

What is your favorite outdoor activity?

Year: _____

_____

_____

_____

_____

Year: _____

_____

_____

_____

_____

Year: _____

_____

_____

_____

_____

September 25

What magazines do you like to read?

Year: _____

_____
_____
_____

Year: _____

_____
_____
_____

Year: _____

_____
_____
_____

September 26

What are your favorite apps?

Year: _____

_____

_____

_____

_____

Year: _____

_____

_____

_____

_____

Year: _____

_____

_____

_____

_____

September 27

What is the strangest food you
have tried lately?

Year: _____

_____

_____

_____

_____

Year: _____

_____

_____

_____

_____

Year: _____

_____

_____

_____

_____

September 28

What were you born to do?

Year: _____

_____

_____

_____

Year: _____

_____

_____

_____

Year: _____

_____

_____

_____

September 29

What is your favorite time of day
to be intimate with your partner?

Year: _____

Year: _____

Year: _____

September 30

What imperfection do you find endearing
in your partner?

Year: _____

_____
_____
_____
_____

Year: _____

_____
_____
_____
_____

Year: _____

_____
_____
_____
_____

October 1

What is one personality difference
between you and your partner?

Year: _____

_____
_____
_____
_____

Year: _____

_____
_____
_____
_____

Year: _____

_____
_____
_____

October 2

Who always has your support?

Year: _____

_____
_____
_____
_____

Year: _____

_____
_____
_____
_____

Year: _____

_____
_____
_____

October 3

What are you trying to fix?

Year: _____

Year: _____

Year: _____

October 4

What rituals make you happy?

Year: _____

_____
_____
_____
_____

Year: _____

_____
_____
_____
_____

Year: _____

_____
_____
_____
_____

October 5

What do you do when no one is watching?

Year: _____

_____

_____

_____

_____

Year: _____

_____

_____

_____

_____

Year: _____

_____

_____

_____

_____

October 6

How many true friends do you have?

Year: _____

_____

_____

_____

_____

Year: _____

_____

_____

_____

_____

Year: _____

_____

_____

_____

_____

October 7

What story do you like to tell?

Year: _____

_____

_____

_____

Year: _____

_____

_____

_____

Year: _____

_____

_____

_____

October 8

What comes up when you
Google your name?

Year: _____

_____

_____

_____

_____

Year: _____

_____

_____

_____

_____

Year: _____

_____

_____

_____

_____

October 9

If you made a toast to your partner,
what would you say?

Year: _____

Year: _____

Year: _____

October 10

What gift would you love to receive today?

Year: _____

_____

_____

_____

_____

Year: _____

_____

_____

_____

_____

Year: _____

_____

_____

_____

_____

October 11

What is your favorite fall activity?

Year: _____

_____

_____

_____

Year: _____

_____

_____

_____

Year: _____

_____

_____

_____

October 12

If you could have any meal today,

what would it be?

Year: _____

_____

_____

_____

_____

Year: _____

_____

_____

_____

_____

Year: _____

_____

_____

_____

_____

October 13

What is your favorite piece of clothing?

Year: _____

_____

_____

_____

_____

Year: _____

_____

_____

_____

_____

Year: _____

_____

_____

_____

October 14

One item on my bucket list is

_____.

Year: _____

_____
_____
_____

Year: _____

_____
_____
_____

Year: _____

_____
_____
_____

October 15

What is the last thing you quit?

Year: _____

_____

_____

_____

Year: _____

_____

_____

_____

Year: _____

_____

_____

_____

October 16

Who thinks you are funny?

Year: _____

_____
_____
_____
_____

Year: _____

_____
_____
_____
_____

Year: _____

_____
_____
_____
_____

October 17

What is your drink of choice?

Year: _____

_____

_____

_____

Year: _____

_____

_____

_____

Year: _____

_____

_____

_____

October 18

Who are you surprised is still your friend?

Year: _____

_____

_____

_____

_____

Year: _____

_____

_____

_____

_____

Year: _____

_____

_____

_____

October 19

Something I need more of in my life is

_____.

Year: _____

_____
_____
_____
_____

Year: _____

_____
_____
_____
_____

Year: _____

_____
_____
_____
_____

October 20

Who is the star of your family?

Year: _____

_____

_____

_____

_____

Year: _____

_____

_____

_____

_____

Year: _____

_____

_____

_____

_____

October 21

What time did you go to bed last night?

Year: _____

_____

_____

_____

_____

Year: _____

_____

_____

_____

_____

Year: _____

_____

_____

_____

_____

October 22

What have you been wanting
to discuss with your partner?

Year: _____

_____
_____
_____
_____

Year: _____

_____
_____
_____
_____

Year: _____

_____
_____
_____
_____

October 23

What does it take to make
a relationship last?

Year: _____

_____
_____
_____
_____

Year: _____

_____
_____
_____
_____

Year: _____

_____
_____
_____
_____

October 24

What worries you lately?

Year: _____

_____

_____

_____

_____

Year: _____

_____

_____

_____

_____

Year: _____

_____

_____

_____

_____

October 25

If you could live in any era,
which one would it be and why?

Year: _____

_____
_____
_____
_____

Year: _____

_____
_____
_____
_____

Year: _____

_____
_____
_____
_____

October 26

When have you helped someone in distress?

Year: _____

_____

_____

_____

_____

Year: _____

_____

_____

_____

_____

Year: _____

_____

_____

_____

_____

October 27

If you could choose one thing to do
differently today, what would it be?

Year: _____

_____

_____

_____

Year: _____

_____

_____

_____

Year: _____

_____

_____

_____

October 28

If you could invite one person to dinner
tonight, who would it be?

Year: _____

_____

_____

_____

_____

Year: _____

_____

_____

_____

_____

Year: _____

_____

_____

_____

_____

October 29

Which philosophy suits you better: "Live
for the moment" or "Plan for the future"?

Year: _____

_____

_____

_____

_____

Year: _____

_____

_____

_____

_____

Year: _____

_____

_____

_____

_____

October 30

What couples' Halloween costume
would you love to wear?

Year: _____

_____

_____

_____

_____

Year: _____

_____

_____

_____

_____

Year: _____

_____

_____

_____

_____

October 31

What scares you the most?

Year: _____

_____

_____

_____

_____

Year: _____

_____

_____

_____

_____

Year: _____

_____

_____

_____

November 1

Do you prefer nights in or nights out?

Year: _____

_____

_____

_____

_____

Year: _____

_____

_____

_____

_____

Year: _____

_____

_____

_____

_____

November 2

When things break, do you
fix them or replace them?

Year: _____

_____

_____

_____

_____

Year: _____

_____

_____

_____

_____

Year: _____

_____

_____

_____

_____

November 3

What are some things that offend you?

Year: _____

_____

_____

_____

_____

Year: _____

_____

_____

_____

_____

Year: _____

_____

_____

_____

_____

November 4

What inspires you?

Year: _____

_____

_____

_____

Year: _____

_____

_____

_____

Year: _____

_____

_____

_____

November 5

When have you felt
protective of your partner?

Year: _____

_____

_____

_____

Year: _____

_____

_____

_____

Year: _____

_____

_____

_____

November 6

What are three things you are willing to
splurge on for yourself?

Year: _____

_____

_____

_____

Year: _____

_____

_____

_____

Year: _____

_____

_____

_____

November 7

How good is your singing?

Year: _____

_____

_____

_____

_____

Year: _____

_____

_____

_____

_____

Year: _____

_____

_____

_____

_____

November 8

What do you fear most about getting older?

Year: _____

_____
_____
_____
_____

Year: _____

_____
_____
_____
_____

Year: _____

_____
_____
_____
_____

November 9

What traditions do you want to start?

Year: _____

_____

_____

_____

_____

Year: _____

_____

_____

_____

_____

Year: _____

_____

_____

_____

_____

November 10

What is your biggest insecurity?

Year: _____

_____

_____

_____

_____

Year: _____

_____

_____

_____

_____

Year: _____

_____

_____

_____

_____

November 11

If you were running for president, what issues
would you build your campaign around?

Year: _____

_____

_____

_____

_____

Year: _____

_____

_____

_____

_____

Year: _____

_____

_____

_____

_____

November 12

What are three things
that you have in common?

Year: _____

_____

_____

_____

_____

Year: _____

_____

_____

_____

_____

Year: _____

_____

_____

_____

November 13

Do you forgive and forget,
or forgive and remember?

Year: _____

_____

_____

_____

_____

Year: _____

_____

_____

_____

_____

Year: _____

_____

_____

_____

_____

November 14

What's a problem you're dealing with now?

Year: _____

_____

_____

_____

_____

Year: _____

_____

_____

_____

_____

Year: _____

_____

_____

_____

_____

November 15

What brightens your day?

Year: _____

_____
_____
_____
_____

Year: _____

_____
_____
_____
_____

Year: _____

_____
_____
_____
_____

November 16

Who or what do you miss the most?

Year: _____

_____

_____

_____

Year: _____

_____

_____

_____

Year: _____

_____

_____

_____

November 17

What do you do when you're upset
with your partner?

Year: _____

_____
_____
_____
_____

Year: _____

_____
_____
_____
_____

Year: _____

_____
_____
_____
_____

November 18

Are you a spender or a saver?

Year: _____

_____

_____

_____

_____

Year: _____

_____

_____

_____

_____

Year: _____

_____

_____

_____

_____

November 19

The holidays make me _____.

Year: _____

_____

_____

_____

_____

Year: _____

_____

_____

_____

_____

Year: _____

_____

_____

_____

_____

November 20

When was the last time you ventured
outside your comfort zone?

Year: _____

_____

_____

_____

_____

Year: _____

_____

_____

_____

_____

Year: _____

_____

_____

_____

_____

November 21

I think I would be happier if I

_____.

Year: _____

_____

_____

_____

_____

Year: _____

_____

_____

_____

_____

Year: _____

_____

_____

_____

_____

November 22

What was the most interesting thing
that happened today?

Year: _____

_____

_____

_____

Year: _____

_____

_____

_____

Year: _____

_____

_____

_____

November 23

What is your idea of success?

Year: _____

_____

_____

_____

Year: _____

_____

_____

_____

Year: _____

_____

_____

_____

November 24

What would you rather not know?

Year: _____

_____

_____

_____

_____

Year: _____

_____

_____

_____

_____

Year: _____

_____

_____

_____

_____

November 25

What positive or encouraging thoughts
have you had today?

Year: _____

_____

_____

_____

_____

Year: _____

_____

_____

_____

_____

Year: _____

_____

_____

_____

_____

November 26

What is one thing that helps your
relationship thrive?

Year: _____

Year: _____

Year: _____

November 27

What are you most thankful for today?

Year: _____

_____
_____
_____
_____

Year: _____

_____
_____
_____
_____

Year: _____

_____
_____
_____
_____

November 28

What makes the two of you a great team?

Year: _____

_____

_____

_____

_____

Year: _____

_____

_____

_____

_____

Year: _____

_____

_____

_____

_____

November 29

How satisfying was your day?

Year: _____

_____

_____

_____

Year: _____

_____

_____

_____

Year: _____

_____

_____

_____

November 30

If you could ask your partner to do one
thing for you today, what would it be?

Year: _____

_____
_____
_____
_____

Year: _____

_____
_____
_____
_____

Year: _____

_____
_____
_____

December 1

My favorite holiday song is

_____.

Year: _____

_____
_____
_____
_____

Year: _____

_____
_____
_____
_____

Year: _____

_____
_____
_____
_____

December 2

What are you longing for?

Year: _____

_____

_____

_____

_____

Year: _____

_____

_____

_____

_____

Year: _____

_____

_____

_____

December 3

If you could change three things about
your home, what would they be?

Year: _____

_____

_____

_____

_____

Year: _____

_____

_____

_____

_____

Year: _____

_____

_____

_____

_____

December 4

What makes you proud of your partner?

Year: _____

_____

_____

_____

_____

Year: _____

_____

_____

_____

_____

Year: _____

_____

_____

_____

_____

December 5

What hopes and dreams
have come true for you?

Year: _____

_____

_____

_____

_____

Year: _____

_____

_____

_____

_____

Year: _____

_____

_____

_____

_____

December 6

If you could go back to school,
what would you want to learn?

Year: _____

_____

_____

_____

Year: _____

_____

_____

_____

Year: _____

_____

_____

_____

December 7

What is one thing you cannot
start your day without?

Year: _____

_____

_____

_____

Year: _____

_____

_____

_____

Year: _____

_____

_____

_____

December 8

If you could go to a concert or
performance, what would it be?

Year: _____

_____
_____
_____
_____

Year: _____

_____
_____
_____
_____

Year: _____

_____
_____
_____

December 9

Would you like to be famous?
If yes, for what?

Year: _____

_____

_____

_____

Year: _____

_____

_____

_____

Year: _____

_____

_____

_____

December 10

What in your life makes you feel grateful?

Year: _____

_____

_____

_____

Year: _____

_____

_____

_____

Year: _____

_____

_____

_____

December 11

If you could wake up tomorrow having gained
one quality or ability, what would it be?

Year: _____

_____

_____

_____

_____

Year: _____

_____

_____

_____

_____

Year: _____

_____

_____

_____

_____

December 12

My partner makes me feel like I'm the only person in the world when he/she _____.

Year: _____

_____

_____

_____

_____

Year: _____

_____

_____

_____

_____

Year: _____

_____

_____

_____

_____

December 13

When was the last time
you were embarrassed?

Year: _____

_____

_____

_____

_____

Year: _____

_____

_____

_____

_____

Year: _____

_____

_____

_____

_____

December 14

How confident do you feel
in your relationship?

Year: _____

_____
_____
_____
_____

Year: _____

_____
_____
_____
_____

Year: _____

_____
_____
_____

December 15

What rules do you break often?

Year: _____

_____

_____

_____

_____

Year: _____

_____

_____

_____

_____

Year: _____

_____

_____

_____

_____

December 16

What makes you feel safe?

Year: _____

_____

_____

_____

_____

Year: _____

_____

_____

_____

_____

Year: _____

_____

_____

_____

_____

December 17

Is life a smooth ride right now
or an off-road adventure?

Year: _____

_____

_____

_____

_____

Year: _____

_____

_____

_____

_____

Year: _____

_____

_____

_____

_____

December 18

My favorite game is _____.

Year: _____

_____

_____

_____

_____

Year: _____

_____

_____

_____

_____

Year: _____

_____

_____

_____

_____

December 19

What friendship is like no other, and why?

Year: _____

_____

_____

_____

_____

Year: _____

_____

_____

_____

_____

Year: _____

_____

_____

_____

_____

December 20

I never learned how to _____.

Year: _____

_____
_____
_____
_____

Year: _____

_____
_____
_____
_____

Year: _____

_____
_____
_____

December 21

What have you accomplished recently?

Year: _____

_____

_____

_____

_____

Year: _____

_____

_____

_____

_____

Year: _____

_____

_____

_____

_____

December 22

My partner is perfect for me because

_____.

Year: _____

_____

_____

_____

_____

Year: _____

_____

_____

_____

_____

Year: _____

_____

_____

_____

_____

December 23

When do you feel most yourself?

Year: _____

_____

_____

_____

_____

Year: _____

_____

_____

_____

_____

Year: _____

_____

_____

_____

_____

December 24

One promise I can make to my partner is

_____.

Year: _____

_____
_____
_____
_____

Year: _____

_____
_____
_____
_____

Year: _____

_____
_____
_____
_____

December 25

What is the best gift you've received?

Year: _____

_____

_____

_____

_____

Year: _____

_____

_____

_____

_____

Year: _____

_____

_____

_____

_____

December 26

What has brought you happiness?

Year: _____

_____
_____
_____
_____

Year: _____

_____
_____
_____
_____

Year: _____

_____
_____
_____
_____

December 27

We will always _____.

Year: _____

_____
_____
_____
_____

Year: _____

_____
_____
_____
_____

Year: _____

_____
_____
_____
_____

December 28

What have you been holding in?

Year: _____

_____

_____

_____

_____

Year: _____

_____

_____

_____

_____

Year: _____

_____

_____

_____

_____

December 29

How much do you enjoy
writing in this journal?

Year: _____

_____
_____
_____
_____

Year: _____

_____
_____
_____
_____

Year: _____

_____
_____
_____
_____

December 30

What is your favorite day from the past year?

Year: _____

_____

_____

_____

Year: _____

_____

_____

_____

Year: _____

_____

_____

_____

December 31

Describe your future together.

Year: _____

_____

_____

_____

_____

Year: _____

_____

_____

_____

_____

Year: _____

_____

_____

_____

_____